I0147493

Rufus Wheelwright Clark

A Discourse Commemorative of the Heroes of Albany

Who have fallen during the present war in defense of our country,

delivered in the North Ref. Prot. Dutch church of Albany, on the evening of

July 10th, 1864

Rufus Wheelwright Clark

A Discourse Commemorative of the Heroes of Albany
Who have fallen during the present war in defense of our country, delivered in the North Ref. Prot. Dutch church of Albany, on the evening of July 10th, 1864

ISBN/EAN: 9783337213343

Printed in Europe, USA, Canada, Australia, Japan

Cover: Foto ©ninafisch / pixelio.de

More available books at **www.hansebooks.com**

A

DISCOURSE

COMMEMORATIVE OF THE HEROES OF ALBANY,

WHO HAVE FALLEN DURING THE PRESENT WAR IN DEFENSE OF OUR COUNTRY,

DELIVERED IN THE

NORTH REF. PROT. DUTCH CHURCH OF ALBANY,

ON THE EVENING OF JULY 10TH, 1864,

By RUFUS W. CLARK, D. D.

———•———

ALBANY:
STEAM PRESS. OF C. VAN BENTHUYSEN.
1864.

CORRESPONDENCE.

ALBANY, July 13th, 1864.

Rev. RUFUS W. CLARK, D. D.:

Dear Sir—A very general desire having been expressed by the relatives and friends of the noble men of our city, who have fallen while defending the liberties and laws of our country, that the discourse you delivered on Sabbath evening, July 10th, in commemoration of their patriotism, valor, and devotion, should be published; we therefore, in behalf of the U. S. Christian Commission, respectfully request that you furnish a copy for publication.   Very truly yours,

    THOMAS W. OLCOTT, *President.*
    JNO. N. RATHBONE, *Vice-President.*
    WM. McELROY, *Treasurer.*
    L. DEDERICK, *Secretary.*

————

ALBANY, July 13th, 1864.

Messrs. THOMAS W. OLCOTT, JOHN F. RATHBONE, WILLIAM McELROY and L. DEDERICK:

Gentlemen—It affords me pleasure to comply with your request; and it will be a gratification to me if you will allow the Discourse to be published for the benefit of the U. S. Christian Commission, an organization which has contributed so largely, to the temporal comfort and spiritual good of our brothers, in the camp and on the battle field.

I take the liberty of adding some sketches and names, that were omitted in the delivery of the discourse.

With the highest respect and esteem, I am truly yours,

    RUFUS W. CLARK.

TO THE

RELATIVES AND FRIENDS OF THE NOBLE PATRIOTS,

OF THE CITY OF ALBANY,

WHO HAVE SACRIFICED THEIR LIVES IN OUR DEFENCE,

AND FOR THE AMERICAN REPUBLIC,

THIS DISCOURSE

IS MOST RESPECTFULLY AND AFFECTIONATELY

INSCRIBED.

DISCOURSE.

2d BOOK OF SAMUEL, i chap., 25 verse.

" HOW ARE THE MIGHTY FALLEN IN THE MIDST OF THE BATTLE."

We bring to you, to-night, a few garlands which we have woven for the illustrious dead. The least that we can do, is, to cherish the memories, and record the deeds of the noble men, who have made sacrifices that we might enjoy tranquility; who have died on the battle field, that we might have peace; who have given their lives for our nation's honor, perpetuity and prosperity. They have done that for us, for which we can never repay them. The debt of gratitude we owe can never be cancelled.

History does not furnish us with an account of any war, which has called forth a purer patriotism, a holier love of liberty, loftier sentiments of honor, duty and devotion to the public good, than have characterized the heroes, who have been engaged, and continued to be engaged, in the struggle for the maintenance of the American nationality. In preserving this nationality they have been inspired with the belief that they were toiling to keep alive the best government that Heaven ever granted to a people; to perpetuate and extend those social, educational and religious institutions, upon which virtue and happiness are based, and to secure the triumph of humanity and justice, over systems of oppression, that are a reproach and a peril to any nation. And on the bright roll of martyr-heroes, none stand higher for purity, bravery, and a lofty patriotism, than those who have gone forth from the city of Albany; and whose precious remains we have followed to the grave, with tears of personal affection, and feelings of the warmest gratitude and admiration. While their cold forms rest with us, their influence and noble deeds have entered into the most valued parts of American history. By dying, they have put fresh life into the republic, and added to the value of our institutions. We have more to love, more to pray for, more to fight for, than we had before their heroism was added to our national character. A republic for which such sacrifices have been made, and upon whose altar such noble and precious lives have been laid, must live, must triumph over all its foes, and shine with new splendor in the ages yet to come.

When first contemplating this tribute to the

departed heroes of our city, it was my purpose to notice all, of whom I could obtain full and satisfactory information. But on investigation, I find the number so large, that to bring my discourse within reasonable limits, I must select a part from the brilliant galaxy of names, that shed their lustre upon our city, and allow them to speak for their comrades, and represent their valor and heroic deeds.

In April, 1861, the first guns were fired from the batteries of treason upon Fort Sumter. The sound of those guns startled the nation, and revealed the existence of a deep, wide spread, and malignant rebellion. After a long period of peace, unity and uninterrupted prosperity—during which the arts had been advanced, the resources of the country developed, manufactures and commerce increased, and the national domain extended, with a rapidity almost without a parallel in history—there burst upon us the storm of war, that now, for more than three years, has been raging, carrying desolation to tens of thousands of homes, and producing an amount of personal suffering, and domestic anguish, that no language can depict.

During the first year of the war several of our families were struck by the lightning from this dark and terrific tempest. Among the dis-

2

tinguished victims, at this early period, there stands out before us the name of Colonel William A. Jackson. The early years of this young hero were passed amid the scenes of a refined, intellectual and christian home. His father, an accurate and distinguished scholar, occupying the Professorship of Mathematics in Union College, Schenectady, quickened by his conversation and instruction the intellect of his son; and the natural talents, as well as mental acquirements of the youth, gave promise of a very successful career in life. In the year 1851 Mr. Jackson graduated at Union College, and some time afterwards he entered upon the profession of law in this city, in partnership with one who is greatly esteemed for his patriotic services, rendered to the government and the country. His frank and prepossessing manners, his quick apprehension of the points of any subject submitted to him for investigation, his power of oratory and varied intellectual attainments, his social relations in the city, and a large circle of friends, rendered his position a most desirable one. But at the call of his country he left all, to vindicate her honor, and defend her against her foes.

It would have been his choice to have died upon the battle field, but exhausted by his toils and anxieties, he was seized with typhus fever, and after a short illness his spirit was called away. He died an honored martyr to our great national struggle for Union and Liberty.

The same year there fell also Sergeant John Waterman, Co. A, 18th regiment; Corporal Thomas Goldwaite, who died at Fort McHenry of typhoid fever; Lieut. Snyder, William Conkling, Robert Cameron, William Cady, a youthful artist who was killed at Great Bethel June, 1861; and the youthful patriot James Rice, the forerunner of another bearing the same name, who, two years afterwards, fell amid a halo of glory, that reflected the brightness of his earthly christian military career, and the lustre of those hopes that guided his pure spirit to mansions in the skies.

Young Rice, of whom we now speak, who died in November, 1861, at Camp King, Munson's Hill, Virginia, was but sixteen years of age when he enlisted to serve his country. The boy left his home inspired with the thought that he, in the hour of the nation's extremity, might do something for our honor or protection. He joined the army with high aims, and proved an active, faithful and efficient soldier. While on picket duty, guarding his companions in arms, he was shot by the enemy and fell. His last words to his dear father were,

"Father I have done my whole duty to my country." And there, before having reached the age of 17, the young hero dies. Though a stranger to us, still we stop to drop the tear of gratitude over his grave, and to commend parents and friends to Him, who can afford consolation under such a bereavement.

Of the citizens of Albany who offered up their lives for their country, during the year 1862, I have the names of twenty, each of whom deserves an extended and earnest tribute. The most illustrious in this company is that of Ormsby Macknight Mitchel; a name dear to many hearts here; one who formerly worshiped within these walls, but who to-day worships in a higher, purer, more glorious temple. Gen. Mitchel was distinguished in so many departments, that I am unable to say whether he was most eminent as an astronomer, a soldier, or a christian. He certainly presented, in a most happy union, scientific culture, earnest patriotism, tender humanity, and devoted piety. His intellect moved among the stars, and caught their brilliancy. His thoughts partook of their harmony and grandeur. His discoveries, and contributions to astronomical science, are alone sufficient to render his name distinguished in the annals of American literature. His popular lectures made him a favorite with all, and inspired the minds of the people with a love for the beauties and sublimities of astronomy, and with adoration for the great Creator, and his marvellous works.

The native genius of an hero appears in the fact, that at the early age of twelve years he had mastered the Latin and Greek languages, acquired the elements of mathematics; and at that time commenced the world for himself as a clerk. For three years he supported himself, and at the age of fifteen went to West Point, with a cadet's warrant, a knapsack upon his back and 25 cents in his pocket. He graduated with honor in 1829, and was at once made assistant Professor of Mathematics, which position he filled for two years. After practicing law in Cincinnati six years, he was elected Professor of Mathematics, Philosophy and Astronomy, at Cincinnati College, which office he filled with distinguished ability for ten years. In 1859 he became director of the Dudly Observatory of this city, and has left here an apparatus for accurate measurements, which bears the impress of his great mechanical skill. But it is with the mechanism of his noble heart, that was nicely adjusted to measure the depths of human suffering; it is with those fine chords that vibrated to the calls of patriotism and the claims of his country; it is with those aspirations that nothing but the truths and glories of christianity could satisfy, that we are chiefly interested. Gen. Mitchel had a soul that could hear the cries of humanity, and respond by toil and sacrifices for the helpless and unfortunate. For the education and happiness of the freedmen committed to his charge, he did what he could ; and at the last great day, many of the recipients of his benevolence, will be ready to rise up and pronounce him blessed. At the moment the breath left his body science lost a rare ornament; the army mourned for a skillful and brave soldier; humanity wept for an earnest defender and advocate ; and the church lost a true christian and humble follower of our Lord Jesus Christ.

Passing along the picture gallery of 1862, we come to another hero who bears the marks of youth, of calm determination, of pure patriotism, and of heroic bravery. He, too, worshipped once within this church and celebrated with you the dying love of Jesus. He was reared and tenderly loved by one whose voice you have often, in years past, heard from this pulpit; but now he sleeps in the battle-field in a soldier's grave, far from parents, sisters and brothers; far from the fond wife, who in youth became a widow; far from a little one who can never look up and say father, but must wait to learn the sad history that makes the child an orphan, and the mother a weeping mourner. You may recognise the portrait as that of Theodore C. Rogers. So noble was his bearing, so manly his bravery, that even the officers of the rebel army, when they saw him leading his soldiers the conflict, gave orders to their own soldiers not to fire at him. And when he fell, by those whom the order did not reach, and his lifeless body was borne from the field and laid under a tree, two generals of the rebel army, while gazing upon him and reading the letters from his parents and wife, taken from his pocket, wept as though a brother of their own had been suddenly hurried into eternity.

During the same year the Fire Department of our city gave up some of its most efficient and useful members for the salvation of the country. Among them we make honorable mention of Lieut. John McCaffrey, of the 104th New York Volunteers, who was formerly foreman of Engine Company No. 12, and at the time he enlisted was a member of company No. 10; of Lieut. James M. Southwick of the 93d Regiment, another brave soldier and efficient officer; of Lieut. James Kin-

near who belonged to company No. 6; men who,
when at home, were ready at any hour of the
night or the day to hasten, the moment the alarm
was given, to protect your houses and property
from the ravages of fire, and then went forth to
lay down their lives for the suppression of that
awful rebellion, that has brought upon our beloved
country such desolation, and carried anguish to
so many hearts.

Col. Edward Frisby, also a brave and noble
officer, was wounded, and then killed by a horse
that was shot and fell upon him. The honors
with which his remains were followed to the
grave in this city, bore testimony to the esteem
and respect in which he was held by a large circle
of friends.

Gladly would we, did time allow, offer an
extended tribute of our gratitude and admiration
to Addison I. Fellows, who just as he was entering upon life, and gaining the esteem and affection
of a large circle of friends, was cut down by the
typhoid fever; to Lieut. Edward Bayard Hill, a
member of the regular service, and a man of
modest bearing, cultivated intellect, and unflinching bravery, who gave his talents, his noble heart,
and his life to his country; to Clarence II.
Stephens, the brave boy of nineteen years, who

fell before the deadly fire of the rebel artillery; to Harmen Visscher, Jr., a youth of excellent attainments and universally esteemed, who was shot through the breast, and was left on the field for dead, but reviving received the attentions of his devoted mother, till the last breath left his body; to Thomas L. Hartness, the brave soldier and devoted Sabbath school teacher; to Lieut. James Reid, the courageous officer, who fell at the fatal battle of Bull Run; to the young James De Lacey, whose affection, as the son of a widowed mother, was equal to his courage upon the battle field, and who fell at the slaughter at Antietam; to the noble and heroic Adjutant John H. Russell; to the brave Robert Caldwell, the only son of a widowed mother; and to Lieut. McCornwell, who fell in the same battle; to George Martin, who after he had passed through all the battles of the Peninsula with Gen. McClellan's army, at last at the battle of Campton Gap was shot through the heart, and leaves a wife and child and a large circle of friends to mourn the loss; to Stephen Ross White, who died of fever at Roanoake Island; also to Edward Augustus Higham, all of whom richly deserve from our hands, and from our citizens, far more than these brief allusions. Mr. Higham when he enlisted was offered a commis-

3

sion, but he replied, "No, the government needs
privates more than officers, and I will go as a
soldier." He went as such, and a more faithful,
self-sacrificing and brave defender of our country
never went into the field. He served under the
lamented and heroic Col. George W. Pratt,
another name, though not strictly classed among
the citizens of Albany, yet one that we cannot
pass without saluting, as deserving of the highest
honors, and of a conspicuous place in the history
of American valor.

Mr. Higham died in the Prince Street Hospital,
Alexandria, Va., Oct. 10, 1862, aged 21 years.
He was a splendid young man, active, intelligent
and upright, with a future exceedingly bright and
promising. He was wounded in the leg at the
battle of Bull Run, August 30th, and left on the
field from Saturday to Monday night, suffering
much from the rain on Saturday night, and the
scorching sun on Sunday. He was taken to the
hospital, where he lingered until his noble spirit
was called to its everlasting rest.

Besides being a brave, conscientious, and patriotic soldier, Mr. Higham was a sincere christian.
He united with the Fourth Presbyterian church of
this city in 1859, at the age of eighteen years;
the church being then under the pastoral care of

the Rev. Dr. Seeley, who took a deep interest in the spiritual welfare of our young hero; and who was very much affected to see the young man come out alone, as he did, to profess his love for Jesus, before angels and men.

The Rev. Dr. McMurdy, chaplain of the hospital at Alexandria, writes of the departed patriot to his fond father, " Your son was a noble young man, patient and uncomplaining in every trouble. He was a sincere and humble christian, and felt that there was no trust but in the mercy of the Redeemer. ' His death is a sacrifice to the country, and may it prove effectual to the nation."

The same year there fell another valued member of the Fourth Presbyterian church. Mr. Whitman Mattoon, the only son of Mr. David Mattoon, who was connected with the 44th regiment, and was killed in the seven days battle on the Peninsula in the early part of July. The particulars of his death have never been received by his afflicted parents, nor has his body been recovered. The precious remains doubtless lie unburied with others of the noble dead; but his brave spirit has gone to that Savior, whom he loved, and labored to serve on the earth.

During the year 1863, scarcely a month passed without some family in our city being plunged into the deepest mourning. And among the offerings made to our county, there were several as distinguished for eminent piety, as for a noble patriotism. I have only to mention, first the name of Adjutant Richard M. Strong, to excite your warmest gratitude and enthusiastic admiration. Fitted by nature, and a superior classical and legal education, to take the highest rank in the profession of law ; qualified to adorn and elevate any social circle that might be favored with his presence ; inspired with a devotion to the cause of Christ that rendered him one of the best of christian counsellors, and the most efficient workers, as his services rendered to the State Street Presbyterian Church, at the period of its organization, can abundantly testify ; he still left all to accept the perils of the battle-field, and the destiny of an American soldier. In collecting his regiment, he underwent great toil and personal sacrifices. He was with his soldiers but a short time before he won their confidence, affections, and admiration. To record his noble deeds, his acts of kindness, and his efforts to lead men to the Savior of the world, would require volumes. Besides his arduous military duties, he acted as chaplain to the regiment, when they were deprived of the services of that officer. He rose early in the morning, and went from tent to tent, and hospital to hospital, ministering to the temporal necessities of the sick and wounded; offering consolation to the sorrowing, and praying with the dying. He was literally broken down by over exertion. His zeal outran his strength. The fires of his patriotism and his piety, consumed the energies of his physical system. At the early age of twenty-eight years his spirit returned to the God who gave it; and to-day Richard M. Strong lives in those blissful regions, where the roar of cannon and the storm of battle are never heard.

Near him the angels may see another hero, who was his co-worker for Christ and for his country on the earth—Lieut. James Williamson of the 177th regiment. Mr. Williamson was one of the first trustees of the State Street Presbyterian Church, and won golden opinions for his efficiency as a church officer, his social qualities, and his high integrity as a business man. His noble traits of character pre-eminently fitted him for the duties of a patriotic soldier, and a braver man never stood before the cannon of the enemy. He was shot through the brain while rallying his men in the "forlorn hope" before Fort Hudson. The orders from the General in command to assail that fort, that citadel of granite and iron, with a

few men, or even a thousand stormers as they
were called, was, in fact, an order for the men to
go directly into their graves. The only visible
prospect before them was instant death, and still
Lieut. Williamson's loyalty and spirit of obedience led him to face even that. Had he been
commanded to go out and fight a lightning storm
with drawn sword, he would doubtless have done
it; and the command would have had just as
much reason and judgment in it, as the command
that cost him his life.

Other of our noble citizens had to bite the dust
before that death giving citadel. Col. M. K.
Bryan, a man full of generous impulses, bravery
and patriotism, who was among the first at the
breaking out of the war to give his services to his
country, and who, for long and weary months,
faithfully discharged the arduous and perilous
duties of his position, fell while gallantly leading
his forces against Fort Hudson.

Step with me a short distance, and look upon
another youthful form lying under a tree gasping
for life. It is the holy Sabbath day, the 14th of
June, 1863, a day when, at least, pious, God fear-
ing soldiers are most reluctant to fight, except in
self-defence. This young officer has been struck
by a shell, which tore away his sword hilt, and

carried it through his left hip. He felt that the assault was well nigh desperate, and all his feelings revolted against a Sabbath day attack upon that strong hold. But obedience and courage are the duties of a soldier, and in no breast did they burn with a purer flame, than in that which is now heaving with its last breath. Far from a christian home, and dear relatives and friends, at 11 o'clock, on that Sabbath, dies Major James Henry Bogart, of Albany, in the 24th year of his age.

When sixteen years of age he united with the church of Christ, and ever lived faithful to his christian vows. As a boy, James was pure minded, truthful, affectionate and obedient. He loved his home, loved his parents and devoted relatives. But he also loved his country; and at the first tidings of rebellion, the spirit of patriotism awoke in his breast, and he consecrated himself to the protection and welfare of his country. His remains lie in the Albany Rural Cemetery, by the side of other heroes, waiting the last trumpet's peal, when to all believers in Jesus, this corruptible will put on incorruption, and this mortal be clothed with immortality.

Another brave soldier who fell at Fort Hudson was Samuel G. Loomis; and to the roll of fame for the year 1863, we must add the names of John Shaffer, a young man of superior worth, who after braving many battles died, and the last words upon his lips were, "My mother;" Charles H. Fredenrich of the 10th regiment, a thorough soldier, greatly beloved by a large circle of friends; Charles H. Haskell, Henry Sayer, Francis Courtney, Geo. G. Thayer, Charles G. Latham, a talented and educated young man, Lieut. S. B. Shepard, Corporal Alonzo E. Lewis, Thomas Edward Cary, who was instantly killed, leaving a father and brother in the army, James McNab, William H. Fields, Lieut. Philips, Capt. Augustus Barker, Bernard Cain, and Christopher G. Burns, who after passing through the dangers of fourteen battles died of consumption, aged twenty-four years.

But we must pause as the trumpet of fame sounds forth the name of Capt. William I. Temple, who fell at the battle of Chancellorsville on Friday, May 1st, 1863. Our city has not given to the war a more brilliant intellect, or more splendid mental attainments than were possessed by this young hero. Though he died just as he was entering upon his twenty-first year, still he lived long enough to prove his power of thought, his capability of rapid acquisition in knowledge, and

his ability to attain the highest rank in any profession, or department of literature or science, to
which he might devote his energies. His genius,
too, seemed to shed its lustre and its refining
influence upon his whole nature. Capt. Temple
was a gentleman of elegant and polished manners,
winning address, and noble and generous impulses.
He partook of the traits of his distinguished father,
Col. Temple, who was governed by a high sense
of honor, as well as a pure patriotism.

At the commencement of the war, Mr. Temple
was a student at Harvard College; and at the call
of his nation, he left all to serve her interests.
He enlisted in the regular army in 1861, and he
gave the fire of his genius, and ardor of his patriotic heart, to the work of subduing the rebellion.
Though but nineteen years of age, he had the
maturity of manhood, the skill of an experienced
officer, and the bravery of a veteran in the service. Officers, who were associated with him,
have said, that they never saw such coolness displayed upon the battle-field as he manifested.
He moved among cannons and exploding shells
with as much ease and calmness, as he would
among a circle of friends in a drawing room. Had
his life been spared, he would doubtless have
dealt some heavy blows upon the monster that is

4

seeking to tear out the vitals of our republic, and the soul of liberty. But in the bloom of youth; in the dawn of his splendid genius, and unconquerable bravery; at the moment the inspiration of a lofty patriotism filled his soul, he fell a martyr to the cause that represents to the world, liberty, education, religion, and all the elements that confer righteousness, peace and happiness upon a nation.

Another name, over which we drop the tear of affection and gratitude, is that of Captain Augustus Barker, the youngest son of William B. Barker, Esq., and grandson of the late William James of this city. He was connected with the 5th New York Volunteer Cavalry, and had distinguished himself in several severe battles. While nobly struggling against the tide of rebellion, he was taken prisoner, and suffered the privations and horrors of the Richmond prisons. But his intense sufferings did not extinguish his patriotism, nor lessen his valor. On regaining his liberty, he devoted himself with fresh enthusiasm to his country; and his manly traits of character, his generosity and courage, made him a favorite with his companions in arms, and with all who knew him.

On the 16th of September, 1863, his regiment

had moved from Hartwood Church to the southern side of the Rappahannock river, while he was left behind in charge of the troops guarding the river. On the next day, while marching to rejoin his regiment, being, at the moment, with a single man in advance of the troops, he was fired upon by guerillas concealed in the adjoining woods. Two balls took effect, one in the right side, and the other in the left breast, each inflicting a mortal wound. He was tenderly cared for, and every thing done to alleviate his intense pains, but he survived his wound but twelve hours.

Thus, at the early age of twenty-two, in the flower of his youth, and in the vigor of his hopes and aspirations, our hero offered up his precious life upon the altar of his country.

Few regiments have suffered more during the war than the 43d New York volunteers, made up principally of Albanians. Previous to May, 1863, this regiment had passed through the battles before Yorktown, Williamsburg, Malvern Hill, Fair Oaks, Seven Pines, Antietam, the second at Bull Run, and each of the battles at Fredericksburg. In the engagement, on the 5th of May, at Fredericksburg, several officers and privates fell, and among them the brave and youthful Capt. Douglass Lodge, who had reached only his

twentieth year. In no breast did the tidings of
the assault upon Fort Sumter, stir deeper or more
patriotic emotions, than in the breast of this young
hero. He was the first volunteer to sign the roll
of a company then forming by Capt. Cottingham;
and although the arrangements for this company
were not perfected, yet he afterwards enlisted in
the 25th regiment, and soon after joined the 43d.
In all the battles to which we have referred, he
greatly distinguished himself, and at Antietam he
won the admiration of his comrades, and for his
gallant conduct was promoted to the Captaincy.
While bravely leading his forces at Fredericksburg, he received a shot in the forehead, and
instantly expired.

From the 177th regiment we were called to
mourn the loss of William Crounse and George
Elder, the latter of whom attended this church
and died from a fever in this city. It was my
privilege to visit this brave youth during his last
days, and to receive from him the testimony of
his love for Jesus, and his trust in the pardoning
mercy of his God. At the early age of eighteen
years, George Elder gave his life for his country,
and to his afflicted parents we tender our warmest
sympathies.

But there is another name dear to the hearts of

many here, and identified with our own church, and the cause of foreign missions, and that is Lieut. William H. Pohlman. This christian hero was born on the Island of Borneo, January 10, 1842, and was the only surviving son of the late Rev. Wm. J. Pohlman, missionary of the American Board to China. He was also a nephew of the late Rev. John Scudder, the devoted and successful missionary to the heathen, who went to India in 1819. Lieut. Pohlman, with his only sister, was sent to the United States at an early age to receive their education; and when the war broke out, he was a member of Rutgers College, in New Brunswick, having entered that institution in the fall of 1859. While quietly and successfully pursuing his studies, preparatory to the gospel ministry, the conviction fastened itself upon his mind, that the country needed his services. For a time he was deeply exercised as to the question of duty, and he laid the subject before God in earnest prayer. Ere long he saw that he must abandon his studies, and fight for his adopted country.

He enlisted as a private in the first New Jersey regiment, May 28, 1861, and very soon displayed the highest qualities of a christian soldier. He passed through all the campaigns with honor,

until January 17th, 1863, when he was promoted
to a Lieutenancy in the 59th regiment, New York
State Volunteers, and shortly after was appointed
acting Adjutant. Wherever duty called him, he
gained the affections and admiration of all his
associates. His purity of life, his lofty patriotism,
and his christian devotion, were, at all times,
conspicuous. After passing through the toil,
hardships and perils of thirteen hard fought battles, he appears before us in the bloody field of
Gettysburg. Our forces weary, hungry and
exhausted by their long marches under the burn-
ing sun, wheeled into ranks to receive the shocks
of the rebel artillery. Those memorable three
days of July, when heroism and brave endurance
won such triumphs, will never be forgotten by a
grateful people. On the 2d of July the valiant
Col. of the regiment was severely wounded, and
Lieut. Pohlman was the only field officer left, during the remainder of the battle. How keenly he
felt his responsibility, and how well he discharged
his duties, his men relate with passionate pride.
How could they falter, when, wherever the peril
was greatest,

"There was no braver sight
Than his young form, steadfast 'mid shot and shell."

But late in the afternoon of Friday, July 3d, a

minie ball struck his arm, and frightfully shattered it. He was at once urged to withdraw from the front, but he answered, "No, never while I have a sound arm left to fight with." An hour later his sword arm failed him, and another ball, glancing from his swordhilt, which it shattered, pierced his right wrist, and severed an artery, thus disabling him from service. At this crisis his noble nature shone forth with new lustre. To the soldiers who would have borne him from the field, now, almost won, he said, " Boys stay in your places. Your country needs every man of you." Thus he left them, but not until he had groped about in his blindness, to recover, if possible, the sword given to him by his adopted mother. Its empty scabbard, battered and bloodstained, with the glorious motto engraved upon it, unmarred : " For God and your country," is now the most cherished relic, to her who filled a mother's place to the orphan boy. He reached the camp, having fainted on the way from loss of blood, and was laid by the side of his beloved Colonel. So careful was he of the feelings of his friends in this city, that he withheld his name from the newspaper reporters, lest the tidings of his wounds might shock those who were dear to his heart

32

In a characteristic note dictated the following day, after first speaking of their glorious victory, he added, " The usual good fortune which has attended me in thirteen battles of the war, has forsaken me in the fourteenth engagement. I bear honorable wounds in my country's cause." Our hero was tenderly cared for, and under the influence of a home presence, and while hoping soon to welcome a beloved only sister, he seemed to rally; but on the night of the 20th he sank rapidly, and at 11 o'clock in the forenoon, July 21st, his noble spirit went to its reward. His nearest relative says of her patriotic and christian brother: "We could not wish him a prouder record, nor ask for him a worthier death.

'Great God of night!
Accept *our* sacrifice ;
Bid thou our country rise,
The joy of longing eyes,
The Home of Right.' "

On entering the gallery for the present year, 1864, we are greeted with another cluster of heroes who reflect the highest honor upon our city, and many of whom combined, in a remarkable degree, the purest christian principles, with the most unselfish patriotism.

The name of Col. John Wilson will ever be held in grateful remembrance, by all the admirers of

the highest type of the Scotch character. This
hero *was a man*, in the full sense of the term.
Splendid and fascinating in appearance; with a
heart full of courage and firmness; with the strong
resolution, and undeviating principles of the old
Scotch covenanters, he went to the battle-field,
and laid his noble life upon the altar of our
country.

Col. Wilson was intimately associated with Col.
Fryer of Greenbush; and they were on the field
together when the brave Fryer was wounded in
the hand. He still continued fighting, until a
shot struck him in the shoulder. Even that did
not drive him from the field; and soon after he
was severely wounded in the lungs, when he was
borne to the hospital. Shortly after, Col. Wilson
was wounded in the leg, and laid by the side of
his friend. The remark was made him: "This
is a great deal to bear." "Yes," replied Col.
Wilson, "*but not too much for the dear old flag.*"*

---

* Since the delivery of this discourse, we have received the melan-
choly tidings of the fall of Col. James D. Visscher, who succeeded Col.
Wilson, in the command of the 43d regiment, N. Y. State Volunteers.
He was killed in the recent fight before the northern defences of Washington.

Col. Visscher was a high minded, courteous gentleman; an unselfish
and warm hearted patriot; a brave man among even the courageous—a
hero among heroes. He rose rapidly in the army, from one position to
another, until he has now risen to the eminence of a martyr for his
country.

Passing along, we come to another countenance
radiant with christian hope, and beaming with
victory. The eyes reveal the inward intelligence.
The lips whisper the peace of the soul. Upon the
brow is stamped, "heroism." In the hand is a
commission addressed to "Brigadier-General
James C. Rice," a name which history will
embalm, and posterity applaud.

Six years ago this hero enlisted under the Captain of our salvation, and professed his faith
before angels and men, in the Madison Square
Presbyterian Church, in the city of New York.
Less than two years ago he took to his heart one,
who is now a widow. She looked and prayed for
the brightness of serene skies, and received the
thunderbolt that has shattered her spirit.

Gen. Rice left this city for the war, as Lieut.
Col. of the 44th regiment. So valuable were his
services, so noble his conduct in the camp and
the field, that he was promoted to the high position that he occupied at his death.

In the last battle that cost him his life, his
bravery and devotion were pre-eminently conspicuous. He went into the battle dismounted,
mingled with his men, cheered them on to the
conflict. So terrible was the storm of battle, that
out of 1800 of his brigade, 857 privates, and 32

officers fell, and still his courage never faltered. After he was struck, and was being borne to the rear, he was met by General Meade, who, on learning the name of the wounded officer, immediately dismounted, and taking him by the hand, expressed the hope that he might soon be healed. Gen. Rice replied that he had little hope of that, but he was ready to give his life for his country. His last letter, addressed to his aged mother, reveals the inner thoughts and workings of his soul. He said, "We are about to commence the campaign, the greatest in magnitude, strength and importance, since the beginning of the war. God grant that victory may crown our arms ; that this wicked rebellion may be crushed, our Union preserved, and peace and prosperity again be restored to our beloved country. My faith, and hope, and confidence are in God alone, and I know that you feel the same. I trust that God may again graciously spare my life, as he has in the past ; and yet we cannot fall too early, if, loving Christ, one dies for his country. My entire hope is in the cross of my Saviour. In this hope I am always happy. We pray here in the army, mother, just the same as at home. The same God who watches over you, also guards me. I always remember you in my prayers, and I know that you never forget me in yours. All that I am, under God, I owe to you, mother. Do you recollect this passage in the Bible, 'Thou shalt keep, therefore, the statutes, that it may be well with thee, and thy children after thee.' How true this is in respect to your children, mother. I hope that you will read the Bible, and trust the promises to the last. There is no book like the Bible for comfort. It is a guide to the steps of the young—a staff to the aged. Well, my dear mother, good bye. We are going again to our duty, to bravely offer up our life for that of our country, and, through God, we shall do it valiantly. With much love and many prayers, that whatever may betake us, we may meet in Heaven at last.

I am your affectionate son,   JAMES."

They will meet again, where sorrow and parting are no more.

On the tablet of your memory, there is engraved another name, which time cannot efface. The lines are cut so deep, that even the ploughshare of a successful rebellion cannot obliterate them. Around the name there might appropriately be the symbols of intense patriotism, unwavering fortitude, and courage that never knew fear. That name is Col. Lewis Benedict. At the battle of Pleasant Hill, up Red river, while gallantly leading his brigade, in the pursuit of the retreating foe, and at the moment the glories of a great victory burst upon him, our hero was pierced by five rebel bullets, and instantly fell, to rise no more. In this engagement he was acting as Brigadier General, and had succeeded in infusing his earnest spirit, and undaunted bravery into the minds of his officers and soldiers; and hurling upon the enemies of God and human freedom, the retribution that they richly deserved. But his zeal always carrying him in into the thickest of the fight; his thought of himself being lost in his love of country, his martyrdom seemed an inevitable fact, to which destiny pointed. It is a wonder that such a hero escaped as long as he did. Col. Benedict was with Gen. Banks in all his battles, and shared largely in his victories. His form was conspicuous in the storming of Fort Hudson; and while that fort poured forth its showers of shell and shot, he stood immovable amid the rain of death, striving to do his duty, and save his men, and his nation.

To the city of Albany belongs the honor of the birth of this distinguished American soldier. He was born of parents of the highest respectability, on the second day of September, 1817. He studied and graduated at Williams College, Williamstown,

Mass., and prepared himself for the profession of law. He held several important offices of trust and responsibility in our city; but when his country was in peril, he left all and rushed to her defense.

In 1861, he was commissioned as Lieut. Col. of the 73d regiment, Excelsior Brigade; and after undergoing the hardships of a soldier, he fought bravely at the battle at Williamsburg. Here he was captured by the enemy, and after several months imprisonment, he was released by exchange. From that time to the hour of his death, he gave his thoughts, energies, valor, and aspirations, to his country's honor and salvation.

The patriotism, also, of William I. Wooley was strikingly conspicuous. He was one of the first to respond to the call of his country, and in spite of ill health, and the remonstrances of friends who felt that his impaired strength rendered him unfit for service, he persevered in his noble efforts for the defense of the nation until his death, which occured in the Georgetown Hospital, July 13, 1861.

We approach next, another hero-martyr, whose remains were recently borne from before this pulpit, to rest in our quiet and beautiful cemetery. In the character of Col. Lewis O. Morris, there was a remarkable combination of tenderness and valor, of kindness and bravery. Whether we look at his gentle attentions as a husband and father, or at his readiness to serve his soldiers or their friends; or at his bravery and splendid achievements upon the battle-field, we are impressed with his pure and noble traits of character.

Col. Morris was born in this city, in August, 1824. He was educated at our academy, and afterwards pursued his studies in Massachusetts. His noble father having been killed at the siege of Monterey, he received a commission in the regular army. At the outbreak of the rebellion, he was in Texas, in command of Fort Brown; and his company was the only one, if we are rightly informed, that did not surrender to the rebels, in that State. So highly was he regarded by the military authorities, that he was appointed to direct the operations against Fort Macon, in North Carolina, which he captured and afterwards commanded. It was a fort of great strength, and its reduction was considered as one of the most brilliant achievements of the war.

In the summer of 1862, Col. Morris was placed in command of the 113th New York regiment, raised in this city, which was the first regiment from this State to arrive in Washington, at the moment when that city was threatened by the rebel army.

When stationed afterwards at Fort Reno, an elegant sword, sash, and belt, were presented to him, in testimony of the affection and admiration of the officers and soldiers, who had experienced the kindness of his noble and generous heart.

Several months before he was killed, he sought with diligence and earnestness an interest in the blessed Saviour, and often conversed with his devoted Chaplain, upon the interests of his immortal soul. And after receiving his death wound, and before he breathed his last, he expressed his love for Jesus, his hope of Heaven, and his readiness to depart and be with Christ.

Two days before the death of Col. Morris, a beloved and honored member of his staff preceded him in the mysterious journey to the spirit land. I allude to the youthful William Emmet Orr, acting assistant Adjutant General, with the rank of First Lieutenant, who was born in this city, September 12th, 1841. His ancestors combined the best, and most vigorous qualities of the Scotch and Irish character; and young Orr partook largely of these elements. In his early childhood he manifested an amiable and lovely disposition, great purity of heart and of life, and was remar-

kable for his obedience and affection as **a son.**
At the age of sixteen years, during a season of
special religious interest, he consecrated himself
to the service of his blessed Saviour, and united
with the Second Presbyterian Church, of this city,
under the pastoral care of the Rev. Dr. Sprague.
He entered upon the christian life with high aims,
and with just views of the nature and obligations
of a public profession of his faith.

He was educated at the excellent school, con-
ducted by the Rev. Mr. Pierson, in Elizabeth,
New Jersey, and was afterwards a student at the
Rochester University. His intellectual attainments, combined with his social and benevolent
traits of character, rendered him a most agreea-
ble companion ; and those who were with him at
Fort Reno, and other places where he was
stationed, speak of him with fondness and
admiration.

Lieut. Orr was also an earnest patriot, and
courageous soldier. One who saw him on the
field, when shot and shell were flying thick around
him, and his comrades were falling, said, that his
bravery could not be surpassed. In the thickest
of the fight, his calm resolution, and fervid and
lofty patriotism never forsook him. He looked

6.

not at danger, but at duty. He asked not for a position of ease and safety, but for one where he could best serve his country, and honor his God.

After spending a night in the rifle pits with Col. Morris, he retired with others in the morning to the woods to take breakfast, when he was shot by a rebel, who fired from a tree. After receiving the fatal wound, he was borne in a rough conveyance forty miles, and was attended by his colored servant on foot, a bright lad of fourteen years, named William Webster, whose mother is a slave at the South. This devoted boy did all in his power for the comfort of our hero; and at every stopping place filled his canteen with fresh water for him. To his attentions Lieut. Orr attributed the prolongation of his life; and the youth is now rewarded by the kind interest of the family, in his welfare and education.

The last few days of Mr. Orr's life, were days of extreme prostration and suffering. He was attended by his devoted parents, who did all in their power for his relief. But on Thursday morning, June 2d, 1864, at one-half past two o'clock, his feet and hands grew cold, his breathing was labored, and in a few moments he bid farewell to his dear friends, his delightful home, his bleeding country, and was attended by the

angels of God, to the mansions prepared for him
in the Heavens by the Saviour, whom he loved.

Among others who deserve our tribute of gratitude, are the honored names of Major William
Wallace, Capt. II. N. Merriman, both brave,
christian soldiers; Capt. Edwin Forrest, George
W. Kilbourn, and Capt. Robert II. Bell, the latter
of whom served with great faithfulness and bravery under the lamented Col. Morris.

We have also another youth, whom nothing but
a sense of duty led to abandon the peaceful pur-
suits of life, and plunge into the perils of the
battle-field. I allude to the young hero, William
A. Van Gaasbeck, who was born in this city,
Sept. 5th, 1841; and who, when 18 years of age,
went to New York to engage in mercantile pur-
suits. Immediately on the news of the first firing
upon Fort Sumter, he wrote to his father, that he
felt it to be his duty to give up his situation, and
enlist in defense of his country. And from that
time up to the 6th of June, 1864, when he was
wounded in the arm, a period of two years and
nine months, he served his country with distinguished bravery and faithfulness. His letters
were always cheerful. He never complained of
the hardships of a soldier's life, and never asked
for a furlough to visit his home and friends. And

even after his arm was taken off at the shoulder, he expressed a hope of a speedy recovery, that he might return again to his battery. But God willed otherwise; and on the 23d of June, he died at Davis Island, near New York, attended by his beloved mother.

William was a truthful, pure minded, affectionate boy. His sense of right and honor were so high, that he could not be tempted to perform a mean or wrong act. The history of his anxieties, sufferings, dangers, and acute pains at the last, are known only to himself and his God.

But there is one other, for whom the tears of sorrow are not yet dry; one whose funeral services are fresh in our memory, the tidings of whose death fell as a thunderbolt upon the hearts of a widowed mother, and a wide circle of relatives and friends. I allude to a child of the covenant, who, in infancy, was brought to the altar, and solemnly dedicated to the Father, the Son, and the Holy Ghost. His name was written in the church books, and in the book of life, Charles E. Pruyn. He was the son of Col. Samuel Pruyn. His footsteps through childhood and youth were followed by christian counsels and fervent prayers. At the beginning of the war, he, actuated by the purest patriotism, bid adieu to the attractions of

home, and went to the battle-field, as a Lieutenant
in the 96th regiment. Very soon it was apparent
that he possessed, in a very eminent degree, all
the qualities of a soldier, a patriot, and a christian.
He said very little about his devotion to his
country, or his willingness to make sacrifices to
maintain our nationality; but three years of
almost unmitigated toil, privation, and suffering,
endured without a single complaint, prove the
spirit of this young officer. His coolness in the
severest conflict; his unflinching bravery, when
soldiers were falling and dying all around him; his
brotherly kindness to the sick and wounded, were
often the subject of remark from his superior
officers, and of expression of deep gratitude from
the recipients of his attentions.

His regiment was in Casey's division; and at
the terrific battle of Fair Oaks was in the advance,
and suffered most severely. Lieut. Pruyn had
just risen from a sick bed, and weak as he was, he
participated in the struggle and dangers of that
fearful encounter. It will be remembered that
that division was severely censured by the General in command; a censure, however, which he
was afterwards compelled to retract. But it had
a cruel effect on the heart of our young patriot.
For him, after all his struggles, and sufferings,

to be branded as a coward, and that too by his commander whom he had almost worshipped, was too much for him. Sick in body, and deeply distressed in spirit, he resigned his commission. But this step he soon regretted, and resolved, before he reached his home, to return to the service. A severe illness, contracted during that dreadful campaign, compelled him to delay any efforts to do so, for several weeks. But before he was sufficiently recovered to leave his room, he was offered the position of Adjutant, in the 118th regiment of N. Y. Vol., then organizing in Plattsburgh. After careful deliberation he accepted the appointment, and left his home when too ill to sit up, more than a few hours at once.

After some months, he was recommended, by the almost unanimous vote of the officers, for the position of Major of the regiment. Though the senior Captain had a superior claim, in the regular line of promotion, still he urged the appointment of Mr. Pruyn, "because he had earned, and deserved the promotion."

A few weeks since, he was badly wounded in the foot, and the surgeon and others urged him to remain in the hospital, as his foot was much inflamed; but he insisted upon being with his noble comrades, and spending all his strength in the service of his country. On the 15th of June, the instant after he had, in a clear, ringing voice, uttered the words, "Attention, Battalion!" preparatory to giving the order "Charge," a shell exploded upon his breast, terribly mangling his body; and with the single exclamation, "Oh!" he expired instantly. He fell at the early age of 23 years. His body was embalmed, and on Monday, June 27th, it was borne, under military escort, to his last resting place, in the Albany Rural Cemetery.

The moral character of our brave and honored townsman was irreproachable. Neither the temptations of the city, nor the trials of camp life, made any inroads upon his lofty principles, and unwavering integrity. When he came back to his home to recruit, he was the same pure minded youth, and tender and affectionate son, that he was when he enlisted to fight the battles of his country.

But it is of his christian character, his abiding confidence in God, and his hope in Jesus Christ, his Saviour, that we delight to speak. At the early age of fifteen, he made a public profession of his religious faith. He entered upon his christian duties, with an earnest desire to be a consistent, faithful, and useful, servant of his

divine master. His recent letters to his fond
mother indicate the growth of his spiritual life.
In one he said: "I have given up all speculations
upon our movements and prospects; where we
are going, and what is before us, I do not know;
but I am happy and contented. I have committed myself fully to the God of battles, and he will
do just what is best for me." His chaplain gave,
also, the most consoling and abundant testimony
to his preparation for the realities of eternity;
and letters received, since his death, from soldiers,
express the warmth of their affection for the
departed.*

---

* The following tribute to his memory has been received since the
delivery of this discourse:

HEADQUARTERS 118th N. Y. S. V.,
IN THE TRENCHES, BEFORE PETERSBURG, Va.,
July 20th, 1864.

Mrs. Mary Pruyn, Albany, N. Y.:

Madam—Enclosed I send you extract from General Orders No. 80,
Headquarters Department Virginia and North Carolina, just received at
these headquarters.

It will assure you that the name of your lamented son is still identified
with the struggle, towards the success of which he contributed his young
life. The nobly fallen have not been forgotten—their memory has been
most fittingly honored.

Along our outer lines their names have been set—gems of encourage-
ment to ourselves—signs of warning to the foe.

It shall be our effort to emulate the brightness of their example—their
devotion—that their sacrifices may prove to have been in behalf of a
cause as gloriously successful as it is gloriously righteous.

I am, Madam, most respectfully,

J. L. CUNNINGHAM,
Captain Commanding 118th N. Y. V.

When such sacrifices are offered up for the
salvation of our country, may we not hope and
believe that God will spare the republic; secure
the triumph of universal liberty; give to us a
future of honor and prosperity; and allow memories like these to be embalmed in the gratitude
and admiration of posterity?

To the bereaved fathers, mothers, widows, and
sisters, before me, we offer our tenderest sympathies, and the consolations of our holy religion.
In the name of the American government and
people; in the name of the christian church, so
intimately identified, as we believe, with our
national history; in the name of the friends of
civil liberty throughout the world, we thank you
for your precious gifts; and it is our fervent
prayer to Almighty God, that you may be prepared to meet the christian heroes who have gone

[*Official.*]
HEADQUARTERS DEPARTMENT OF VIRGINIA AND NORTH CAROLINA. }
IN THE FIELD, Va., July 15th, 1864. }
General Orders No. 80.

In honor of the memory of some of the gallant dead of this army, who
having fallen in this campaign, the redoubts and batteries on the lines
will hereafter be known as follows, viz:— *   *   *   *   *
Battery No. 6 is named Battery Pruyn, after Major Charles E. Pruyn,
One Hundred and Eighteenth New York Volunteers. *   *   *   *
By command of   Major Gen. B. F. BUTLER.
(Signed)   R. S. DAVIS,
Major and Assistant Adjutant General.

7

before you, to those blissful regions, over which the Prince of peace reigns ; and where the blessings of loyalty and love, are the portion of all the subjects of the Supreme and Glorious King.

www.ingramcontent.com/pod-product-compliance
Lightning Source LLC
Chambersburg PA
CBHW031810090426
42739CB00008B/1235

* 9 7 8 3 3 3 7 2 1 3 3 4 3 *